I0813836

OH MY GOD, KENNY'S ALIVE!

First published in 2025 by OH
An Imprint of HEADLINE PUBLISHING GROUP LIMITED

1

Disclaimer:
This book has not been licensed, approved, sponsored, or endorsed by anyone involved in the creation, production or distribution of *South Park* television series.

Cataloguing in Publication Data is available from the British Library

ISBN 978-1-03542-302-6

Compiled and written by: Jason Ward
Editorial: Saneaah Muhammad and Stella Caldwell
Designed and typeset in Avenir by: Stephen Cary
Project manager: Russell Porter
Production: Marion Storz
Printed and bound in Dubai

Headline's policy is to use papers that are natural, renewable and recyclable products and made from wood grown in well-managed forests and other controlled sources. The logging and manufacturing processes are expected to conform to the environmental regulations of the country of origin.

HEADLINE PUBLISHING GROUP LIMITED
An Hachette UK Company
Carmelite House, 50 Victoria Embankment, London EC4Y 0DZ

The authorised representative in the EEA is Hachette Ireland, 8 Castlecourt Centre, Dublin 15, D15 XTP3, Ireland (email: info@hbgi.ie)

www.headline.co.uk www.hachette.co.uk

OH MY GOD, KENNY'S ALIVE!

THE LITTLE GUIDE TO SOUTH PARK

UNOFFICIAL AND UNAUTHORIZED

CONTENTS

INTRODUCTION – 6

8
CHAPTER ONE
SCREW YOU GUYS!

38
CHAPTER TWO
PRETTY FUCKED UP

68
CHAPTER THREE
YOU BASTARDS!

98
CHAPTER
FOUR
M'KAY?

128
CHAPTER
FIVE
WHAT, WHAT, WHAT?

158
CHAPTER
SIX
HOWDY, NEIGHBOR!

INTRODUCTION

Howdy, neighbors – welcome to South Park!

Satirical and scatological, profane and profound, absurd and amoral, *South Park* is a wet dream for anyone who, like the show's pioneering creators Trey Parker and Matt Stone, sees the despicable hypocrisy in pop culture and takes great glee in punching up (and down) to take out those responsible. It's ridiculously funny too – and has been consistently so for nearly 30 years.

Often regarded as one of the greatest TV shows ever made, *South Park*'s legacy has defied all the odds – its humor has defined a generation (or three) and its depraved subject matter has defiled and warped our fragile little minds, all in the best possible way. For our continued viewing pleasure, Kyle, Stan, Cartman, Kenny (and Trey and Matt, too) have yet to grow up – allowing us to hold onto our child-like sense of wonder about a fucked-up world that never disappoints.

Enjoy!

THE FOLLOWING GUIDE CONTAINS COARSE LANGUAGE, AND, DUE TO ITS CONTENT, SHOULD NOT BE READ BY ANYONE. M'KAY?

CHAPTER ONE

SCREW YOU GUYS!

South Park is an ensemble comedy, but the breakout star is 10-year-old Eric Cartman. Across more than 300 episodes, Cartman has been guilty of more crimes than it's possible for any one child to commit – murder, theft, arson, prostitution, cannibalism, war crimes, animal abuse, grave robbery, piracy, embezzlement, terrorism, drug possession, smuggling and armed robbery – and we still can't get enough of him.

So, three cheers for the boy, the brat and the obnoxious psychopath – Cartman!

"Follow your dreams, and you can reach your goals; I'm living proof."

Eric Cartman

I looked in my mom's closet and saw what I was getting for Christmas. An UltraVibe Pleasure 2000!

”

Cartman, on his mom – and her plan to be naughty at Christmas.

Season 1, Episode 9, "Mr. Hankey, the Christmas Poo"
31 of the Funniest South Park Jokes and Quotes, inews.co.uk

I've learned something too: selling out is sweet because when you sell out, you get to make a lot of money, and when you have money, you don't have to hang out with a bunch of poor asses like you guys. Screw you guys, I'm going home.

Cartman, on his successful Mr. Hankey T-shirts, and making money from them when Hollywood comes to town.

Season 2, Episode 9, "Chef's Chocolate Salty Balls"
Eric Cartman's Best Quotes in South Park, Ranked, cbr.com

I want to get down on my knees and start pleasing Jesus. I want to feel his salvation all over my face.

”

Cartman, on pleasing Jesus, and his Christian rock band, Faith+1.

Season 7, Episode 9, "Christian Rock Hard"
Cartman's Best Lines, IGN.com

Well, excuse me, Kyle, for trying to keep some optimism, sometimes when things seem their darkest, you just need to try and stay… HIV positive, but if you want to be so HIV negative all the time…

Cartman, to Kyle and Stan, after he's infected with HIV because doctors botched his tonsil surgery, but remaining "HIV-positive about it" – much to Kyle's anger.

Season 12, Episode 1, "Tonsil Trouble"
Top 10 Funniest Cartman Quotes on South Park, watchmojo.com

Words cannot express how much I hate you guys!

”

Cartman, driven by spite, leads a Confederate army of Civil War reenactors to revive the Confederacy just to avoid losing a bet with Stan and Kyle about which side won America's Civil War.

Season 3, Episode 14, "The Red Badge of Gayness"
Top 10 Funniest Cartman Quotes on South Park, watchmojo.com

No, no, Kyle, don't be so hard on yourself.

”

Cartman, to Kyle, after Kyle states he's a Jew.

***South Park: Bigger, Longer & Uncut* (1999)**
South Park: Bigger, Longer & Uncut Funniest Moments, tvtropes.org

If you want to find some quality friends, you have to wade through all the dicks first.

”

Cartman, looking for new friends online on Chat Roulette, but finding only (literal) dicks.

Season 14, Episode 4, "You Have 0 Friends"
South Park's Best Quotes, quotecatalogue.com

I would never let a woman kick my ass. If she tried anything, I'd be like, 'HEY! You get your bitch ass back in the kitchen and make me some pie!...' Be a man, Stan. Just say, 'Hey, woman, you shut your mouth and make babies.'

Cartman, to Stan, after Stan receives a black eye from his sister Shelly after she beat him up.

Season 1, Episode 5, "An Elephant Makes Love to a Pig"
The 10 Best Eric Cartman Quotes from South Park, Ranked, collider.com

This is a bunch of crap! I've been lickin' this carpet for three whole hours and I don't feel like a lesbian.

”

Cartman, to Stan and Kyle, about what it takes to become a lesbian.

Season 1, Episode 11, "Tom's Rhinoplasty"
Best South Park Quotes, needsomefun.net

Love is like taking a dump, Butters. Sometimes it works itself out. But sometimes you gotta give it a nice, hard, slimy push.

Cartman, on love, after a new girl, Nichole, arrives at school.

Season 16, Episode 7, "Cartman Finds Love"
Top 10 Funniest Cartman Quotes on South Park, watchmojo.com

You will respect my authoritah!

”

Cartman,* after becoming a deputy police officer and the power goes to his head.

Season 2, Episode 3, "Chickenlover"
Top 10 Funniest Cartman Quotes on South Park, watchmojo.com

* "There's nothing worse than Cartman with authoritah!" Stan says in "Tweek vs. Craig" (Season 3, Episode 5)

"Mom! Ben Affleck is naked in my bed!"

Cartman, tricked by his own hand (named Mitch Conner) into believing he is dating Jennifer Lopez (who he is obsessed with) and also Ben Affleck's girlfriend.

Season 7, Episode 5, "Fat Butt and Pancake Head"
Cartman's Best Lines, IGN.com

“It’s definitely easier to take the truth in animated form. It might be hard to make live-action little kids dying funny. That would be difficult to do, even with special effects. But since it’s a cartoon, we can control these kids in a way you never could with a real kid. We can make them act the way real kids act.”

Trey Parker, on why *South Park* is animated, interview with David Wild, *Rolling Stone*, January 13, 2015.

Look, these perverts aren't going to rest until they've made love to one of us, right? So, one of us is just going to have to go out there and take one for the team. And I think in all fairness, it should be Butters.

”

Cartman, on Internet predators he meets online after joining the "North American Man/Boy Love Association" (NAMBLA).

Season 4, Episode 5, "Cartman Joins NAMBLA"
Cartman's Best Lines, IGN.com

I kinda always thought you were my best friend.

”

Cartman, to Kenny, in a rare moment of poignancy... though, not really.

Season 5, Episode 13, "Kenny Dies"
South Park: Cartman's 20 Funniest Quotes, screenrant.com

I am nothing like *Family Guy!* When I make jokes, they are inherent to a story – deep, situational and emotional jokes based on what is relevant and has a point! Not just one random, interchangeable joke after another!

”

Cartman, on the animated show *Family Guy.*

Season 10, Episode 3, "Cartoon Wars, Part I"
Cartman's Best Lines, IGN.com

Fuck off, you donkey-raping shit eater.

”

Cartman, under the clear influence of the Terrance and Phillip's potty-mouthed movie *Asses of Fire*.

***South Park: Bigger, Longer & Uncut* (1999)**
South Park: Bigger, Longer & Uncut, moviemistakes.com

Oh, the tears of unfathomable sadness. Mmmm, yummy! Yummy you guys!... Nyahnyahnyahnyah nyah nyah! I made you eat your parents! Nyahnyahnyahnyah nyah nyah!

Cartman, after forcing Scott Tenorman to eat his recently deceased parents (disguised as a nice bowl of chili), and then licking his tasty tears.

Season 5, Episode 4, "Scott Tenorman Must Die"
The 10 Best Eric Cartman Quotes from South Park, collider.com

One time, my cousin and I touched willies. I didn't say that! Yes I did, but why?

”

Cartman, pretending he has Tourette's Syndrome.

Season 11, Episode 8, "Le Petit Tourette"
Eric Cartman's Best Quotes in South Park, Ranked, cbr.com

"Much like the breast cancer patients, I too have something I'd like to get off my chest."

Cartman, mocking Wendy Testaburger's breast cancer awareness presentation.

Season 12, Episode 9, "Breast Cancer Show Ever"
Best South Park Quotes, needsomefun.net

"If I knew where Mel Gibson was, I'd be down on my knees licking his balls."

Cartman, on his obsession with Mel Gibson's *Passion of the Christ*.

Season 8, Episode 3, "Passion of the Jew"
Cartman's Best Lines, IGN.com

I checked on the Internet, Kyle, and getting Butters to put my wiener in his mouth wouldn't make me not gay like you said!

Cartman, trying to prove his heterosexuality in the only way he knows how.

Season 11, Episode 2, "Cartman Sucks"
Cartman's Best Lines, IGN.com

Life goes by pretty fast. If you don't stop and look around once in a while, and do whatever you want all the time, you could miss it.

”

Cartman, misquoting Ferris Bueller (who was quoting John Lennon).

Season 12, Episode 7, "Super Fun Time"
Eric Cartman's Best Quotes in South Park, Ranked, cbr.com

Stan, don't you know the first law of physics? Anything that's fun costs at least eight dollars.

”

Cartman, on the first law of physics.

Season 9, Episode 12, "Trapped in the Closet"
Cartman's 20 Funniest Quotes, screenrant.com

For two billion dollars
I could handle my grandpa's
balls, Sir.

Cartman, on getting rich.

Season 7, Episode 13, "Butt Out"
All the Times Eric Cartman Said Exactly the Right Thing, ranker.com

What's to understand? You get a boner, slap her titties around some and then stick it inside her and pee. Unless you don't want to get her pregnant, then you pull it out and pee on her leg.

”

Cartman, on sex with a woman.

Season 10, Episode 10, "Miss Teacher Bangs a Boy"
All the Times Eric Cartman Said Exactly the Right Thing, ranker.com

I don't make the rules, Ma'am, I just think them up and write them down.

”

Cartman, to a crack whore about making money from her crack whore baby.

Season 15, Episode 5, "Crack Baby Athletic Association"
South Park: Cartman's 20 Funniest Quotes, screenrant.com

I'm killing you. But unfortunately, I could only afford a wiffle bat, so it's going to take a while.

Cartman, to Kyle, attempting to beat Kyle to death.

Season 7, Episode 3, "Toilet Paper"
Eric Cartman's Best Quotes in South Park, Ranked, cbr.com

CHAPTER TWO

PRETTY FUCKED UP

Loosely based on the personality of the show's co-creator Trey Parker, fourth-grader Stan Marsh is the most logical, sensitive and patient of the Four Boys. He often serves as the moral compass of the deeply amoral show – though, like his hilarious father, Randy, Stan is not without his eccentricities.

Stan, over to you, my boy…

"Dude, this is pretty fucked up right here."

Stan Marsh

Parents can be pretty cruel sometimes, dude. They get off on it.

”

Stan, on parents.

Season 4, Episode 16, "The Wacky Molestation Adventure"
South Park: Stan's 10 Funniest Quotes, screenrant.com

Cartman, that isn't cool. You shouldn't joke about Kenny being dead. Enough time hasn't passed... We have to wait 22.3 years before we can joke about it.

Stan, on killing Kenny, after Cartman jokes, "You're deader than Kenny!"

Season 6, Episode 1, "Jared Has Aides"
The Best Stan Marsh Quotes from South Park, ranker.com

Renting DVDs is more ancient than Madonna's boobs!

”

Stan, on Madonna's boobs.

Season 16, Episode 2, "Cash For Gold"
The Best Stan Marsh Quotes from South Park, ranker.com

Dude, girls' volleyball isn't a joke; jokes are hard and require skill.

Stan, on girls' volleyball.

Season 18, Episode 8, "Cock Magic"
The Best Stan Marsh Quotes from South Park, ranker.com

In 2001, *South Park: Bigger, Longer & Uncut* earned a Guinness World Record for having the most profanity used in an animated film.

It has a total of 399 swear words, including 146 uses of the word "fuck," 199 offensive gestures and 221 acts of violence.

I thought I was having a great time because I was getting signed by managers and... going to big sex and coke parties, but then I realized... I was having fun because I was doing all that with my best friend.

Stan, after becoming a Guitar Hero legend at the expense of his friendship with Kyle.

Season 11, Episode 13, "Guitar Queer-O"
South Park: Most Insightful Stan Quotes, gamerant.com

Bullying is an ugly thing. We should beat its ass until it starts to cry.

”

Stan, on bullying bullying.

Season 16, Episode 5, "Butterballs"
South Park: Most Insightful Stan Quotes, gamerant.com

"

Stan says you're a cont, *cont, cont...*

"

Jimmy Valmar, to Wendy Testaburger, after Stan asks Jimmy to ask Wendy out for him. Jimmy was meant to say, "Stan says you're a continuing source of inspiration to him," but his stutter makes it sound like "cunt". Wendy replies, "Tell Stan to fuck off!"

Season 7, Episode 14, "Raisins"
31 of the Funniest South Park Jokes and Quotes, inews.co.uk

You're not really my friend, you're just a guy who hangs out with me all the time. ”

Stan, to Kyle, questioning the depth of their friendship.

Season 15, Episode 8, "Ass Burgers"
45 Funny South Park Quotes with Iconic Humor for a Good Laugh, trstdly.com

Art is just kinda for gaywads.

”

Stan, on art.*

Season 7, Episode 2, "Krazy Kripples"
Stan Marsh (South Park), thyquotes.com

* Butters replies, "But I love our class!" This prompts Stan to respond, "See?!"

Dude, how do you tell if a piece of poo is in trouble?

”

Stan, to Kyle, when Mr. Hankey, the Christmas poo, becomes deathly ill.

Season 2, Episode 9, "Chef's Chocolate Salty Balls"
Stan Marsh (South Park), thyquotes.com

"

You can say that again, Kenny.

"

Stan, to Kenny, when Kenny says "Mmffm mmfmm mmmfmmm."

Season 1, Episode 11, "Tom's Rhinoplasty"
Stan Marsh Quotes, southparkquotes.com

America may have some problems, but it's our home, our team. And if you don't wanna root for your team, then you should get the hell out of the stadium.

”

Stan, on America (Fuck Yeah!).

Season 5, Episode 9, "Osama bin Laden Has Farty Pants"
Stan Marsh Quotes, southparkquotes.com

Jesus, is it okay to kill somebody if they ask you to? Because they're in a lot of pain, you know, like assisted suicide?

Stan, to Jesus Christ, who replies, "My son, I wouldn't touch that with a 60-foot pole."

Season 1, Episode 6, "Death"
South Park: Stan's 10 Funniest Quotes, screenrant.com

What's a muff cabbage?

Stan, on vaginas (presumably).

Season 14, Episode 7, "It's a Jersey Thing"
The Best Kyle Broflovski Quotes from South Park, Ranked, ranker.com

Competing against other people and getting in their faces saying 'Haha! I'm better than you!' is part of life.

”

Stan, on life.

Season 8, Episode 4, "You Got F'd in the A"
South Park: Stan's 10 Funniest Quotes, screenrant.com

Hey, guys. Do you know where I can find the clitoris?

Stan, on the clitoris. Cartman replies, "What, is that like finding Jesus or something?"

***South Park: Bigger, Longer & Uncut* (1999)**
South Park: Bigger, Longer & Uncut Quotes, moviequotes.com

"

I *am* socializing, retard! I'm logged onto an MMORPG with people from all over the world and getting XP with my party using team speak!

"

Stan, to his father, Randy, after spending all weekend on the computer playing games.

Season 10, Episode 8, "Make Love, Not Warcraft"
Stan Marsh Quotes, wikiquote.org

No, Jay Leno's chin is big-boned. You are a big fat ass.

”

Stan, to Cartman, about his big boned-ness.

Season 1, Episode 3, "Weight Gain 4000"
South Park Quotes, imdb.com

Well, we're going to go work on getting Kyle's dad an erection.

Stan, to Randy, on Kyle's dad's erectile dysfunction.

Season 3, Episode 2, "Spontaneous Combustion"
35 South Park Quotes to Revisit Their Iconic Misadventures, quoteambition.com

Yeah, whatever, ya fat bitch.

Stan, to Ms. Crabtree, hoping she heard him say, "I have a bad itch."

Season 1, Episode 1, "Cartman Gets an Anal Probe"
Stan Marsh Quotes, QuoteCatalog.com

Stanley, you call your friend an asshole this instant, like a normal kid!

”

Randy Marsh, to Stan, after Stan called Cartman a "big silly goose".

Season 5, Episode 2, "Cripple Fight"
15 Out-of-Context Quotes and Jokes from South Park, cracked.com

Well, at least my mom isn't on the cover of *Crack Whore* magazine.

”

Stan, on Cartman's mom, after the boys found out she appeared in *Crack Whore* magazine.

Season 1, Episode 7, "Pinkeye"
Stan Marsh Quotes, thyquotes.com

You mean, at one point in this guy's life, he decided he wanted to work up people's butt holes?

”

Stan, on proctologists.

Season 7, Episode 1, "Cancelled"
30+ Hilarious South Park Quotes to Boost Your Fan "Authoritah", scarymommy.com

"Whoa, wait a minute! What did I do wrong? I haven't even talked to Wendy for weeks!"

Stan, to Bebe Stevens, after she tells Stan that Wendy Testaburger is breaking up with him.

Season 7, Episode 13, "Raisins"
Stan Marsh Quotes, thyquotes.com

Sometimes the things we do don't matter right now. Sometimes they matter later. You have to care more about later sometimes, you know?

Stan, on the consequences of his behavior.

Season 2, Episode 12, "Kenny Dies"
35 South Park Quotes to Revisit Their Iconic Misadventures, quoteambition.com

Tom Cruise locked himself in my closet and he won't come out.

”

Stan, after Tom Cruise (literally) locks himself in the closet.

Season 9, Episode 12, "Trapped in the Closet"
South Park: Most Insightful Stan Quotes, gamerant.com

Dude, don't you have enough? I mean, you got tons of money, a jet, and the biggest rock band in the world, a hot wife, and you've been knighted. I mean, at some point, can't you just kind of fuck off?

”

Stan, to U2's lead singer, Bono.

Season 11, Episode 9, "More Crap"
Season 11 Quotes, wikiquote.org

CHAPTER THREE

YOU BASTARDS!

As the only Jewish kid in South Park, Kyle Broflovski stands alone, particularly in the eyes of Eric Cartman – though thankfully he stands his ground.

Alongside Stan, Kyle is the voice of reason in the show, intelligent and empathetic – though not without his own fiery temper and desire to flirt with utter chaos.

He's a good kid, though. This one's for Kyle…

"Oh my god, you killed Kenny, you bastards!"

Kyle Broflovski

He must have a huge bone in his ass, then.

”

Kyle, to Mrs. Cartman, after she claims, "Eric isn't fat, he's big-boned."

Season 3, Episode 10, "Korn's Groovy Pirate Ghost Mystery"
The Best Kyle Broflovski Quotes from South Park, Ranked, ranker.com

Mom! Dad! I have awesome news! The doctor who gave Mr. Garrison a sex-change said he could make me tall and black!

Kyle, on the great things about cosmetic surgery.

Season 9, Episode 1, "Mr. Garrison's Fancy New Vagina"
Kyle Broflovski Quotes, southparkquotes.com

Kenny McCormick's demise was a running gag in *South Park*'s early seasons, occurring in nearly every episode. No matter the situation, he'd inevitably meet a gruesome end, prompting Stan and Kyle's now-iconic reaction, "Oh my God! They killed Kenny! You bastards!"

The line is actually a meta-jab at the show's creators, Trey Parker and Matt Stone, who confirmed the outburst is directed at them for repeatedly killing off Kenny.

Across the series and *South Park: Bigger, Longer & Uncut*, Kenny has died more than 100 times!

You can't say 'fuck' in school, you fucking fat ass!

”

Kyle, to Cartman, for saying "fuck" at school.

***South Park: Bigger, Longer & Uncut* (1999)**
The Best Kyle Broflovski Quotes from South Park, Ranked, Ranker.com

"

Cartman, you don't buy pubes, you grow them yourself!

"

Kyle, after Cartman claims to have bought pubes.

Season 5, Episode 4, "Scott Tenorman Must Die"
Kyle Broflovski Quotes, southparkquotes.com

We never thought it was gonna get on television, let alone become a worldwide phenomenon. But to still exist after all these years is a major accomplishment. But to still be relevant? That's epic.

Les Claypool, lead singer of Primus and composer of the show's iconic theme tune, on the beginning of *South Park*, interview by Ryan Faughnder, *Los Angeles Times*, August 9, 2022.

You sold us out?! For an iPod Nano?!

”

Kyle, to Stan, after he sold out the group by signing them up to go ziplining – a terrible idea, as it turns out – all for a free Nano.

Season 1, Episode 6, "I Should Have Never Gone Ziplining"
The Best Kyle Broflovski Quotes from South Park, Ranked, ranker.com

"

Mr. Hankey, the Christmas Poo. Haven't you guys ever heard of it?

"

Kyle, on Mr. Hankey, the Christmas Poo.

Season 1, Episode 9, "Mr. Hankey, the Christmas Poo"
Kyle Broflovski Quotes, southpark.fandom.com

This is about more than fart jokes! This is about freedom of speech, about censorship and stuff.

”

Kyle, on freedom of speech, censorship and stuff.

***South Park: Bigger, Longer & Uncut* (1999)**
The Best Kyle Broflovski Quotes from South Park, Ranked, ranker.com

Dude, I think it might be best for us to never piss Cartman off again.

Kyle, to Stan, after Cartman gets his sweet revenge on ninth grader Scott Tenorman.

Season 5, Episode 4, "Scott Tenorman Must Die"
The Best Kyle Broflovski Quotes from South Park, Ranked, ranker.com

Who needs hospitals and insurance when we have TikTok and YouTube?

”

Kyle, on trying to navigate the American health system.

The End of Obesity (2024)
South Park: 10 Best & Funniest Quotes from *The End of Obesity* Special, screenrant.com

We're guys, dude. We find something about all our friends to rip on. We made fun of you for being rich for the same reason we rip on Butters for being wimpy. And Stan for being in love with Wendy. And Cartman for being fat. And Cartman for being stupid. And Cartman for having a whore for a mom. And Cartman for being a sadistic asshole.

Kyle, on Cartman.

Season 14, Episode 6, "201"
Kyle Broflovski Quotes, imdb.com

I believe that you believe you helped write that joke. That's how people like you work. Your ego is so out of whack that it will do whatever it can to protect itself. And people with a messed-up ego can do these mental gymnastics to convince themselves they're awesome, when really, they're just douchebags!

Kyle, to Cartman, after Cartman claims he wrote the world-famous "fishsticks" joke – when he was simply just in the room when it was written.

Season 15, Episode 5, "Fishsticks"
South Park Quotes, southpark.fandom.com

What part of being infected with a *deadly* disease do you find funny? Stop saying that you're not just sure, *you're* HIV-positive! This isn't funny, AIDS isn't funny, dying isn't funny, so shut the fuck up!

”

Kyle, to Cartman, who uses his HIV diagnosis as a way to be funny.

Season 12, Episode 1, "Tonsil Trouble"
30+ Hilarious South Park Quotes to Boost Your Fan "Authoritah", scarymommy.com

30 BILLION*

The total number of minutes fans of the show watched in 2019, according to Comedy Central – making it one of the top 10 most-watched shows in the world.

* To watch all 325+ episodes of the show, including specials and movies, would require more than 7,584 minutes, or 127 hours.

So, Jesus died and then three days later he had an erection?

”

Kyle, on Jesus's *resurrection* (presumably).

Season 3, Episode 2, "Spontaneous Combustion"
Kyle Broflovski Quotes, southparkquotes.com

Cartman, that's the dumbest thing you've ever said... this week.

Kyle, to Cartman, after Cartman says, "If you eat food and crap out your butt, then maybe if you stuck food up your butt, you would crap out your mouth."

Season 6, Episode 8, "Red Hot Catholic Love"
Kyle Broflovski Quotes, imdb.com

Do you guys know why no one else at school likes hanging out with you? Because you're always doing stuff like this. You're always coming up with some stupid idea to do something, and then it backfires, and then you end up in some foreign country, or in outer space or something. That's why no one likes hanging out with you guys.

”

Craig Tucker, on Kyle, Stan and Cartman's stupid behavior – in this instance, forming a Peruvian flute band.

Season 10, Episode 12, "Pandemic"
South Park Quotes, tvtropes.org

Over the past few months, I have watched you go from an ancillary character with a few amusing catchphrases to a dried-out spooge rag covered in the jizz of a thousand older men. ”

Kyle, to Towelie, whose crippling drug use has spiraled out of control.

Season 14, Episode 7, "Crippled Summer"
The Best Kyle Broflovski Quotes from South Park, Ranked, ranker.com

GODDAMNIT, don't you get it?! I hate pee! I'm grossed out by pee! The only thing I find more *disgusting* than pee… is *bananas*!

”

Kyle, on pee… and bananas.

Season 13, Episode 11, "Dances with Smurfs"
Season 13 South Park Quotes, wikiquote.org

Wait, wait, I think I can explain this whole thing. Marklar, these Marklars want to change your Marklar. They don't want this Marklar or any of his Marklars to live here, because it's bad for their Marklar. They use Marklar to try and force Marklars to believe their Marklar. If you let them stay here, they will build Marklars and Marklars, they will take all your Marklars and replace them with Marklar...

These Marklars have no good Marklar to live on Marklar, so they must come here to Marklar. Please, let these Marklars stay where they can dwell and prosper without any Marklars, Marklars or Marklars.

”

Kyle, on Marklars, an intelligent species of identical aliens that use the word "Marklar" to refer to all people, places, ideas and things.

Season 3, Episode 13, "Starvin' Marvin in Space"
The Best Kyle Broflovski Quotes from South Park, Ranked, ranker.com

I've been thinking: How did shamelessness get to this? Did it start with fat people on scooters? Or did it start way before that? And then I started thinking: maybe it was us. I don't know, but maybe somehow we lowered the bar, a long time ago. And now we're all sitting here, in the stink of it all. There's no going back, Stan.

”

Kyle, having an existential crisis about the shamelessness of humanity.

Season 15, Episode 7, "You're Getting Old"
The Best Kyle Broflovski Quotes from South Park, Ranked, ranker.com

NO! I don't wanna look like this! I can hide it! Nobody ever *has* to know! I can't ever let anybody know!

Kyle, after his mom tells him that he is "technically from Jersey".

Season 14, Episode 9, "It's A Jersey Thing"
The Best Kyle Broflovski Quotes from South Park, Ranked, ranker.com

Family isn't about whose blood you have in you. Family's about the people who cared about you and took care of you. We're not the same blood, but I love my little brother. We've taken care of him because he needed us to, and that makes us more family than anything.

Kyle, on the importance of family and his beloved little brother, Ike.

Season 7, Episode 15, "It's Christmas in Canada"
35 South Park Quotes to Revisit Their Iconic Misadventures, quoteambition.com

I've learned something today. You see, the basis of all reasoning is the mind's awareness of itself. What we think, the external objects we perceive, are all like actors that come on and off stage. But our consciousness, the stage itself, is always present to us.

Kyle, on logical reasoning – to which Cartman replies, "Tits."

Season 4, Episode 1, "The Tooth Fairy's Tats"
The Best Kyle Broflovski Quotes from South Park, Ranked, ranker.com

Dude, you don't understand. I'm a Jew. I have a few hangups about killing Jesus.

Kyle, to Jesus, shortly before Jesus asks Kyle to stab him in the neck.

Season 11, Episode 5, "Fantastic Easter Special"
The Best Kyle Broflovski Quotes from South Park, Ranked, ranker.com

I learned something today... terrorizing people works.

Kyle, on the magical power of threatening people with violence.

Season 14, Episode 6, "201"
The Best Kyle Broflovski Quotes from South Park, Ranked, ranker.com

CHAPTER FOUR

M'KAY?

After three seasons in Third Grade, the Four Boys grow up – sort of. They move to Fourth Grade, where they've been stuck ever since – for more than 25 years!

In that time, they've been lectured by an insane asylum of teachers, chefs, adults and idiots who are just as ill-behaved as they are.

Welcome to Fourth Grade…

"'Fuck' is the worst word that you can say, so just use the word, 'm'kay'"

Mr. Mackey

When I get a chipotle blue-cheese bacon burger at Bennigan's, I forget all about my dad being queer and my mom trying to kill me. I'm going to be okay.

Butters, lying to himself about his situation at home.

Season 5, Episode 14, "Butters' Very Own Episode"
Butters Stotch, southparkquotes.com

Lu Lu Lu, I've got some apples.
Lu Lu Lu, you got some too.
Lu Lu Lu, let's get together.
I know what we can do,
Lu Lu!!

Butters, and his famous song about apples.

Season 8, Episode 4, "You Got F'd in the A"
South Park: Butters' 10 Funniest Quotes, screenrant.com

"

Mrrph rmph rmmph mrrphh!

"

Kenny, on, er, mrrph rmph rmmph mrrphh.

Season 7, Episode 10, "Grey Dawn"
Kenny McCormick Quotes, southparkstudios.co.uk

Mom, Dad, I love you. Please don't sell me to Paris Hilton.

”

Butters, to his parents, after Paris Hilton tries to buy him to be her new pet after the last one shot itself.

Season 8, Episode 12, "Stupid Spoiled Whore Video Playset"
South Park: Butters' 10 Funniest Quotes, screenrant.com

Let me assure you there is nothin' funny about going up to a nice clean unsuspectin' urinal, m'kay, droppin' your pants, then turnin' around, squattin' over that urinal, m'kay, maybe... maybe pullin' your butt cheeks apart with your hands, m'kay, and then layin' down a big fudge dragon for all the world to see.

Mr. Mackey, on going "dookie" in the urinal.

Season 10, Episode 9, "The Mystery of the Urinal Deuce"
The Best Mr. Mackey Quotes from South Park, Ranked, ranker.com

It's when you take your finger and you stick it in a vagina and you stick it in again and again.

”

Kenny, on fingerbanging, and what precisely it is.

Season 4, Episode 8, "Something You Can Do With Your Finger"
Season 4 Quotes, wikiquote.org

No – I have arms and legs and everything.

Butters, replying to Wendy Testaburger's insult "Are you just an asshole?"

Season 17, Episode 10, "The Hobbit"
Butters Stotch Quotes, southpark.fandom.com

Eric Cartman's name was inspired by Matt Karpman, a friend of the creators known for his sharp comebacks and obnoxious attitude.

During a 1995 Super Bowl party, Karpman's high-five attempt was met with, "Shut up, Karpman!" Trey Parker immediately declared, "Cartman! That's the perfect name for the fat kid."

What the hell is that? Oh my God! What is that thing?! Children, there's some huge bulbous monstrosity heading for the classroom! Oh my God, it's awful! It's coming for the door.

Mr. Garrison, on American comedian Rosie O'Donnell.

Season 4, Episode 12, "Trapper Keeper"
The Best Mr. Garrison Quotes from South Park, Ranked, ranker.com

Boys, I seriously doubt that Mr. Garrison ever said, uh, 'Eat penguin shit, you ass-spelunker.'

Mr. Mackey, on Mr. Garrison.

***South Park: Bigger, Longer & Uncut* (1999)**
South Park: Bigger, Longer & Uncut Funniest Moments, tvtropes.org

> Oh My God! They killed Cartman!

Kenny, to Stan and Kyle, after Cartman is trampled to death by cows.

Season 2, Episode 13, "Cow Days"
Kenny's 10 Best South Park Quotes, Ranked, cbr.com

Now, wait a minute. I wanna clear the air here. We all know that pigeon was a whore. Raise your hand if you didn't sleep with that pigeon?

Mr. Garrison, on making love to that pigeon.

Season 3, Episode 1, "Jakovasaurs"
The Best Mr. Garrison Quotes from South Park, ranker.com

In the beginning, we were all fish swimming around in the water. One day, a couple of fish had a retard baby. And the retard baby was different, so it got to live. So, the retard fish goes on to make more retard babies, and then one day, a retard baby crawled out of the ocean with its mutant fish hands. And it had butt sex with a squirrel or something and made this retard frog squirrel.

And then that had a retard baby, which was a monkey-fish-frog. And then this monkey-fish-frog had butt sex with that monkey, and that monkey had a mutant retard baby that screwed another monkey, and that made you. So, there you go – you're the retarded offspring of five monkeys that had butt sex with a fish squirrel. Congratulations.

”

Mr. Garrison, on evolution, "a bunch of bull crap"

Season 10, Episode 12, "Go God Go"
Line-O-Rama: Mr. Garrison's Best Lines, IGN.com

I die all the time! ALL THE TIME! And you assholes NEVER remember!!

”

Kenny, as alter-ego superhero Mysterion, to the Boys, about Kenny's countless deaths.

Season 14, Episode 13, "Coon vs. Coon & Friends"
Kenny McCormick Quotes, southparkstudios.co.uk

Why did the pigeon cross the road? Because it was having sex with the chicken.

”

Jimmy Valmar tells a joke to make an angry Cartman laugh.

Season 5, Episode 10, "How to Eat With Your Butt"
South Park: Jimmy's 10 Funniest Quotes, screenrant.com

So many of the songs are about our balls that it's hard to keep them straight.

Trey Parker, reflecting on the subject matter of the show's songs, interview by Ryan Faughnder, *Los Angeles Times*, August 9, 2022.

We never want to repeat ourselves. There's definitely tropes, but for it to be funny, it's got to be new. Just going, 'Cartman is fat, and he likes cheesy poofs' is not going to make us laugh.

Trey Parker, on keeping the comedy fresh, interview by Ryan Faughnder, *Los Angeles Times*, August 9, 2022.

The economy is so bad; a picture is now only worth 200 words.

”

Jimmy Valmar, on the U.S. economy, and a solid satirical joke.

Season 16, Episode 1, "Reverse Cowgirl"
South Park: Jimmy's 10 Funniest Quotes, screenrant.com

We always come back to *South Park*. It's always there for us. We definitely want to go do other shit in life, whether it's creative or just travel or whatever. We always want to do a movie, but movies are so hard to get going. We did Broadway and that was an amazing experience. But then you come back, and there's those four boys, and it's like we don't have to go into startup mode.

Matt Stone, on his enduring love for Kyle, Kenny, Stan and Cartman, interview by Ryan Faughnder, *Los Angeles Times*, August 9, 2022.

I want to stick my balls inside your rectum, Kyle. I'm gonna make love to your asshole, children. Kenny, how would you like to sodomize my black ass?

”

Chef, in song, after his return to South Park after a long hiatus – and there's something different about him (see above).

Season 10, Episode 1, "The Return of Chef"
Chef Quotes, southparkquotes.com

Hello, class, I'm Ms. Choksondik.

Diane Choksondik, the Boys' new fourth-grade teacher, whose name says it all.

Season 4, Episode 11, "Fourth Grade"
South Park Quotes, tvtropes.org

I'm very happy to get this award, but you know what makes me happier? Sucking balls.

”

Mr. Garrison, making an acceptance speech for sticking a gerbil up the butt of Mr. Slave.

Season 6, Episode 14, "Death Camp of Tolerance"
Line-O-Rama: Mr. Garrison's Best Lines, IGN.com

You're not from the IRS! You glued my pubes onto your face!

Scott Tenorman, to Cartman, after selling him his pubes.*

Season 5, Episode 4, "Scott Tenorman Must Die"
Best South Park Quotes, needsomefun.net

* A crime for which Cartman makes him pay – by making Scott eat his own dead parents.

> Just listen to this, children: DRUGS ARE BAD. Don't even try to find out about them. Remember, there's a time and place for everything… it's called college.

Chef, to the Boys, after Mr. Mackey passes round a joint in class – and it mysteriously disappears.*

Season 2, Episode 3, "Ike's Wee Wee"
31 of the Funniest South Park Jokes and Quotes, inews.co.uk

* Mr. Garrison stole it and was later seen watching *Teletubbies* while high.

“

What the hell is going on here? Why won't anyone pound Mr. Slave's tight butt?

”

Mr. Garrison, at a nightclub, after everyone in South Park becomes a metrosexual, and being gay is no longer different.

Season 7, Episode 8, "South Park is Gay!"
The Best Mr. Garrison Quotes from South Park, ranker.com

“

TIMMIH!

”

Timmy, his iconic catchphrase.

Season 4, Episode 3, "Timmy 2000"
Timmy Burch Quotes, southparkstudios.co.uk

Kyle, every boy pays for kisses. Do you know what I am saying? If you've got a girl, and she kisses you, sooner or later you're paying for it. You've gotta take her out to lunch, take her to a movie, and then spend time listenin' to all her stupid problems. Look at Stan. Why he's gotta sit there and listen to her stupid motherfuckin' problems 'cause she kisses him.

Butters, to Kyle, about girls, after Kyle expresses interest in being kissed by one.

Season 13, Episode 9, "Butters' Bottom Bitch"
Best South Park Quotes, needsomefun.com

CHAPTER FIVE

WHAT, WHAT, WHAT?

South Park is a show where modern life is seen through the eyes of a motley crew of foul-mouthed kids.

But let's not blame them for everything – their parents (and so-called guardians) are often the ones responsible for the most reprehensible behavior on display – much of which is pure comedy gold.

Adults, what do you have to say for yourselves?

"I've never been able to say this before, but... I love you, son."

Randy Marsh

Don't talk back, Butters, go to your room! I don't know what's wrong with that boy. It can't be our parenting, we're awesome! He must have some kind of mental illness.

Stephen Stotch, on his son, Butters – who is later misdiagnosed with multiple personality disorder.

Season 15, Episode 6, "City Sushi"
South Park Quotes, imdb.com

We just promised ourselves we'd never make a movie for the sake of making a movie, which is why we never took a multi-picture deal. If we have a great idea, we'll go, 'Oh, this could be a cool movie.' Or really for us, it's more like, 'Oh, this is a really bad idea. Let's do this. This seems really stupid.'

Trey Parker, on whether there will ever be a sequel to 1999's *South Park* movie, interview with Jeff Otto, IGN, May 19, 2012.

Fuck you! Let me talk to him, you bitch! I'm not high! I haven't been high since Wednesday. Oh, oh, it is Wednesday?

Towelie, to his wife, who won't let Towelie talk to his son when high.

Season 14, Episode 7, "Crippled Summer"
The Best 25 Towelie from "South Park" Quotes, Ranked, ranker.com

To get the pre-pubescent voices of Kyle, Stan, Kenny and Cartman just right, grown men Matt Stone and Trey Parker use audio software to pitch the kids' voices up by three semitones.

“

I stuck a gerbil up your ass and they want to give me a goddamn medal!

”

Mr. Garrison, trying to get himself fired for being gay (so he can sue for sexual discrimination) by inserting the class pet – a gerbil named Lemmiwinks – into the anus of his lover, Mr. Slave.

Season 6, Episode 14, "The Death Camp of Tolerance"
South Park Quotes, imdb.com

As you get older, boobs will start becoming a major part of your life. But you can't let them get in the way of your friends. There are a lot of boobs out there. But they're just boobs; your friends are forever. I know you think this set of boobs is important now, but those boobs will be replaced by another set of boobs. Boobs will come and go, and then, someday, you'll meet a pair of boobs that you want to marry. And those become the boobs that matter the most.

Randy Marsh, to Stan, on love and romance… and boobs.

Season 6, Episode 10, "Bebe's Boobs Destroy Society"
31 of the Funniest South Park Jokes and Quotes, inews.co.uk

If Saddam Hussein is making weapons then we have to stop him... with our weapons.

”

Randy Marsh, to Sharon Marsh and the South Park townsfolk.

Season 6, Episode 12, "A Ladder to Heaven"
South Park Quotes, Imdb.com

Dag-nabbit children! How come every time you come in here you've got to be asking me questions I shouldn't be answering? 'Chef, what's a clitoris? What's a lesbian, Chef? How come they call it a rim job, Chef?' For once, can't you kids come in here and say, 'Hey Chef, nice day isn't it?'

Chef, to the Boys, before being asked something deeply inappropriate.

Season 4, Episode 15, "Fat Camp"
Best Chef Quotes from South Park, Ranked, ranker.com

Ms. Cartman, eight years old is a little late to be considering abortion.

Abortion Clinic Receptionist, to Liane Cartman.

Season 2, Episode 2, "Cartman's Mom is Still a Dirty Slut"
South Park Quotes, southpark.fandom.com

Ooh! I thought a group of Vietnamese people were having their intestines pulled out through their mouths.

Randy Marsh, to Stan, after hearing Stan's band rehearse in the garage.

Season 7, Episode 9, "Christian Rock Hard"
Randy Marsh Quotes, imdb.com

Hey, everybody, have you seen my balls? They're big and salty and brown. If you ever need a quick pick-me-up, just stick my balls in your mouth. Ooooo, suck on my chocolate salty balls, put 'em in your mouth.

Chef, singing "Chocolate Salty Balls".

Season 2, Episode 9, "Chef's Chocolate Salty Balls"
The Best Chef Quotes from South Park, Ranked, ranker.com

I'm not chugging beer! I'm sampling a flight of gluten-free German lagers with a French wine pairing! It's called a smörgåsvein and it's elegantly cultural!

”

Randy Marsh, on his love of craft beer (any beer).

Season 18, Episode 6, "Freemium Isn't Free"
31 of the Funniest South Park Jokes and Quotes, inews.co.uk

How come you always want to make love to me from behind? Is it because you want to pretend I'm somebody else?

Satan, to Saddam Hussein, who replies, "Satan, your ass is gigantic and red. Who am I going to pretend you are, Liza Minelli?"

***South Park: Bigger, Longer & Uncut* (1999)**
South Park: Bigger, Longer & Uncut Quotes, moviequotes.com

It's when you put your legs behind your head and have someone lick your ass.

Liane Cartman, answering Sheila Broflovski's question, "What the heck is a rimjob?"

***South Park: Bigger, Longer & Uncut* (1999)**
South Park: Bigger, Longer & Uncut, Funniest Moments, tvtropes.org

Don't lie, Stan. Lying makes you sterile.

”

Mr. Garrison, to Stan, after Stan passes a note to Kyle in class.

Season 2, Episode 12, "Clubhouses"
30+ Hilarious South Park Quotes to Boost Your Fan "Authoritah", scarymommy.com

“Well, I'm sorry, Wendy, but I just don't trust anything that bleeds for five days and doesn't die.”

Mr. Garrison, to Wendy Testaburger, a child, about women.

***South Park: Bigger, Longer & Uncut* (1999)**
Line O Rama: Mr. Garrison's Best Lines, IGN.com

During the opening theme tune, composed and performed by American alt-rock band Primus, Kenny can be heard singing muffled lyrics that change slightly throughout the first 10 seasons:

"I like girls with big fat titties, I like girls with deep vaginas!"
(Seasons 1, 2)

"Me, I got a 10-inch penis, use your mouth if you wanna clean it." (Seasons 3, 4, 5)

"Someday I'll be old enough to stick my dick up Britney's butt!"
(Seasons 7, 8, 9, 10)

"I like fucking silly bitches and I know my penis likes it."
(Season 10 to present)

There was a ghost! And, uh... this is ectoplasm! It ran through here... and slimed me.

”

Randy Marsh, caught in a "compromising" position at his computer,* and covered in white goo.

Season 12, Episode 6, "Over Logging"
31 of the Funniest South Park Jokes and Quotes, inews.co.uk

* Randy was masturbating to "Japanese girls puking in each other's mouths", FYI

Sure, Vietnam was fun, but not going-to-the-circus fun or fly-fishing-in-Montana fun. It was more shoving shards of broken glass up your ass and then sitting in a tub of Tabasco sauce fun.

Jimbo Kern, on his time spent in Vietnam, but not on holiday.

Season 2, Episode 6, "The Mexican Staring Frog of Southern Sri Lanka"
Jimbo Kern Quotes, southparkquotes.com

You've got to hold the football like you would hold your lover. Gently, yet firmly. You wanna be both nurturing and clinging at the same time. Oh, yes. Just like making sweet love to the football. Be naughty with the football. Mmmm, spank it. Ever so gently. Spank it. Oh, uh, sorry, children.

”

Big Gay Al, teaching the kids football in his own style.

Season 1, Episode 4, "Big Gay Al's Big Gay Boat Ride"
Big Gay Al Quotes, southparkquotes.com

Don't you see, gingers? If you don't want to be made fun of anymore, all you need are guns and bombs to get people to stop.

”

Jesus Christ, on gingers, in the infamous episode "201", which was censored, threatened and banned.

Season 14, Episode 16, "201"
Best Kyle Broflovski Quotes from South Park, Ranked, ranker.com

Hey! We don't say 'fuck' at the table, you little asshole.

Stuart McCormick, to Kenny, after saying "fuck".

Season 2, Episode 10, "Chickenpox"
Stuart McCormick Quotes, southparkquotes.com

We're in the business of making people go, 'What the fuck is this?'

”

Trey Parker, on the motivation behind creating *South Park*, interview with David Wild, *Rolling Stone*, January 13, 2015.

Do you like putting fishsticks in your mouth?

Jimmy Valmer, to Cartman, on the infamous joke that famously "Kanye West" didn't get.

Season 15, Episode 5, "Fishsticks"
South Park Quotes, southpark.fandom.com

Well, I know a little kitty who is sleeping with mommy tonight.

”

Liane Cartman, after Cartman refers to his pet Kitty as "being a dildo".

Season 1, Episode 1, "Cartman Gets an Anal Probe"
South Park Quotes, newschoolers.com

We accidentally replaced your heart with a baked potato. You have about three seconds to live.

Dr. Gouache, talking to Kenny at the hospital. The doctor was voiced by George Clooney.

***South Park: Bigger, Longer & Uncut* (1999)**
South Park: Bigger, Longer & Uncut Quotes, moviequotes.com

What seems to be the officer, problem?

”

Randy Marsh, after being pulled over by a police officer for drink driving.

Season 9, Episode 14, "Bloody Mary"
South Park: 10 Absolutely Hilarious Randy Marsh Quotes, screenrant.com

Horrific, deplorable violence is okay, as long as people don't say any naughty words! That's what this war is all about!

Sheila Broflovski, reminding the townspeople why she started a war on Canadian trash-talking TV starlets, Terrance and Philip.

***South Park: Bigger, Longer & Uncut* (1999)**
South Park: Bigger, Longer & Uncut Quotes, moviequotes.com

CHAPTER SIX

HOWDY NEIGHBOR!

South Park is filled with famous faces and humble folks all around (and ample parking day and night), so we couldn't resist offering up a smörgåsbord – or smörgåsvein, as Randy says – of the very best wit and wisdom from the Park's ever-growing community of creeps, crazies and crackpots.

So, leave your woes behind and, once again, come on down to South Park…

"DUDE! What the FUCK?"

Kenny McCormick

You so much as touch Kitty's ass, and I'll put a firecracker in your nut sack and blow your balls all over your pants.

Cartman, protecting his beloved Kitty, after fireworks are banned in South Park.

Season 2, Episode 8, "Summer Sucks"
Best South Park Quotes, needsomefun.com

“

They took our jobs!

”

South Park residents, whenever a local job is taken by a non-local – it's a running joke.

Season 8, Episode 7, "Goobacks"
45 Funny South Park Quotes with Iconic Humor for a Good Laugh, trstdly.com

You see, boys, a woman is sensitive in her vagina and it feels good to have a man's penis inside of it. But sometimes a woman chooses to use other things. Telephones, staplers, magazines. It's because the nerve endings in the vagina are so sensitive, it's like a fun tickle.

Sheila Broflovski, to Stan, on the wonder of 69s, and other forms of lovemaking.

Season 6, Episode 14, "The Return of The Fellowship of The Ring to the Two Towers"
South Park Quotes, imdb.com

Wait a minute! You're supposed to poop on the toilet facing out? But I thought you sit on the toilet so that you have that nice little shelf for your comics and chocolate milk? No? Oh jeez, that's embarrassing.

Butters, to Kyle, on his unique pooping technique.

Season 16, Episode 1, "Reverse Cowgirl"
45 Funny South Park Quotes with Iconic Humor for a Good Laugh, trstdly.com

We did an appearance at UCLA recently. All these kids asked us, 'Where did you get the idea for this episode? And where did you get the idea for that story?' And we were like, 'Acid. Acid and, uh, acid.'

Trey Parker, on the inspiration behind the show's story ideas, interview with David Wild, *Rolling Stone*, January 13, 2015.

I run with 12 gangs, and we only commit hate crimes. Whatever! I'll do what I want!

”

Cartman, on joining a new gang (after he gets kicked out of the gang when Bebe Stevens develops boobs – and the Boys lose their minds).

Season 6, Episode 3, "Freak Strike"
Best South Park Quotes, needsomefun.com

Weeeeell, Kyle's mom's a bitch, she's a big fat bitch, she's the biggest bitch in the whole wide world!

Cartman, on Kyle's mom (according to Cartman).

***South Park: Bigger, Longer & Uncut* (1999)**
South Park: Bigger, Longer & Uncut Funniest Moments, tvtropes.org

Alright, let's hear it for Kyle! He's so funny, isn't he guys?! With all his jokes about Cartman being poor. You guys hear how poor Cartman's mom is?! His mom is so poor, the ducks throw bread at her! Hahaha! Yeah, that's super funny, guys! Cartman's mom is so poor that when she goes to KFC, she has to lick other people's fingers! Hahah!

Cartman, after learning he is the poorest kid in the school, after Kenny.

Season 15, Episode 14, "The Poor Kid"
Cartman Quotes, southpark.fandom.com

A blowjob isn't with your mouth, it's with your heart. Now get on your knees and put that heart to work.

"Steven Sondheim" sings Randy Marsh's subtext-less "Splooge-Drenched Blowjob Queen" song, written after Randy learns the all-powerful secret to musicals.*

Season 15, Episode 11, "Broadway Bro Down"
South Park Quotes, thyquotes.com

* Women give blowjobs after seeing them, apparently.

I can't wait for our first shore leave so I can get me some fucking poontang. ”

Mr. Garrison, confirming that his transformation into a whoremongering army soldier is now complete.

***South Park: Bigger, Longer & Uncut* (1999)**
South Park: Bigger, Longer & Uncut Quotes, moviequotes.com

I can't lose weight, Butters, because I'm not fat, I'm big-boned. You can't slim down bones, stupid!

Cartman, to Butters, about his weight.

Season 6, Episode 1, "Jared Has Aides"
Eric Cartman, southparkquotes.com

Your mother was worried sick… and I've been watching TV.

”

Randy Marsh, to Stan, after Stan's late return from the Park's County Pee Wee hockey team.

Season 10, Episode 14, "Stanley's Cup"
Best South Park Quotes, needsomefun.com

“

I’m not a monkey,
I’m a woman!

”

Mr. Garrison, on evolution.

Season 2, Episode 13, “12 Monkeys”
Best South Park Quotes, needsomefun.com

How would you feel, if someone came into your home, m'kay? And pulled down their pants and laid a big mud monkey right on your mom's face?

Mr. Mackey, on, er, um, mud monkeys.

Season 10, Episode 9, "The Mystery of the Urinal Deuce"
Best South Park Quotes, needsomefun.com

Mom, if you were in a German 'scheisse' video, you'd tell me, right?

Cartman, to his mom, after seeing her in a niche German porn video. She replies nonchalantly, "Sure, hon."

***South Park: Bigger, Longer & Uncut* (1999)**
South Park: Bigger, Longer & Uncut Quotes, moviequotes.com

Now, because white people say, 'hizzle fo shizzle,' we have to say, 'flippity floppity floop!'

Chef, to Mr. Garrison, offering advice on what he did when white people stole his culture.

Season 7, Episode 8, "South Park is Gay!"
15 Out-of-Context Quotes and Jokes from South Park, cracked.com

Kenny's family is so poor, they took out a second mortgage on their cardboard box.

Cartman, on poor ol' Kenny.

Season 1, Episode 7, "Pinkeye"
Eric Cartman, Southparkquotes.com

'Hey there, Butters, would you like to slap my titties around?'...'No thanks Ma'am, I'll get in trouble again.'

Butters, in conversation with a Barbie doll.

Season 3, Episode 8, "Two Guys Naked in a Hot Tub"
Best South Park Quotes, needsomefun.com

I am super, thanks for asking!

Big Gay Al, after Stan's gay dog, Sparky, runs away to Big Gay Al's Big Gay Animal Sanctuary.

Season 1, Episode 4, "Big Gay Al's Big Gay Boat Ride"
45 Funny South Park Quotes with Iconic Humor for a Good Laugh, trstdly.com

An episode of *South Park* can be made, from scratch to completed show, in just six days.* In 30 years, only one episode has missed its broadcast – Season 17's "Goth Kids 3: Dawn of the Posers" (Episode 4). An unexpected power outage at Parker and Stone's studio was to blame, which resulted in the episode airing a week later.

*It takes *Family Guy* 10 months to produce one episode. Just sayin'.

It's a man's obligation to stick his boneration in a women's separation; this sort of penetration will increase the population of the younger generation.

”

Cartman, to Stan and Kyle, on his favorite psalm, while in church.

Season 4, Episode 9, "Do The Handicapped Go to Hell?"
Best South Park Quotes, needsomefun.com

How come everything today has involved things either coming in or going out of my ass?

Cartman, on his anal probe.

Season 1, Episode 1, "Cartman Gets an Anal Probe"
Eric Cartman Quotes, Southparkquotes.com

“

How would you like to suck my balls, Mr. Garrison?

”

Cartman, to Mr. Garrison, after Cartman says the word "fuck" during class – which leads to a whole thing.

***South Park: Bigger, Longer & Uncut* (1999)**
South Park: Bigger, Longer & Uncut Quotes, moviequotes.com

Goddammit, Butters, what did I say about shooting guys in the dick?

Cartman, to Butters, after an incident at P. F. Chang's.

Season 12, Episode 8, "The China Probrem"
Best South Park Quotes, needsomefun.com

You know, Mom, the least you could do is kiss me first because I like to get kissed before I get fucked.

Cartman, to his mom, after she didn't buy him an iPad from Best Buy.

Season 15, Episode 1, "HUMANCENTiPAD"
Best South Park Quotes, needsomefun.com

Intelligent and friendly... on rye bread with some mayonnaise.

”

Cartman, to Stan, about dolphins, though he may have them confused with Eskimos.

Season 1, Episode 3, "Weight Gain 4000"
South Park Quotes, newschoolers.com

Tolkien, how many times do we have to go through this. You're black. You can play bass.

”

Cartman, about Tolkien's role in his Christian rock band – and his fondness for using black stereotypes.

Season 7, Episode 9, "Christian Rock Hard"
What's Your Favorite Quote From South Park?", twistedsifter.com

When a chick says, 'We need to talk,' you might as well start punching yourself in the balls, dude.

”

Cartman, to Stan, about Stan's girlfriend, Wendy Testaburger.

Season 14, Episode 10, "Insheeption"
30+ Hilarious South Park Quotes to Boost Your Fan "Authoritah", scarymommy.com

There's more germs on most furniture than there is in pee. If anything, you should wash your hands before you touch your wiener.

”

Butters, speaking the truth about washing your hands before having a pee.

Season 13, Episode 14, "Pee"
Best South Park Quotes, needsomefun.com

“Well, you see, Eric, sometimes when a man and a woman are attracted to each other, they want to be close to each other... And sometimes the man puts his hoo-hoo dilly in the woman's cha-cha.”

Liane Cartman, to Cartman, about the identity of his father. Cartman responds, "So who put his hoo-hoo dilly in your cha-cha?" (The answer, of course, was *who didn't*?)

Season 1, Episode 13, "Cartman's Mom is a Dirty Slut"
South Park Quotes, imdb.com

Beating off the dog is not appropriate when we have company. Uh, I mean ever. Beating off the dog is not appropriate, ever.

”

Randy Marsh, to Stan, about poor ol' Sparky.

Season 5, Episode 7, "Proper Condom Use"
Best South Park Quotes, needsomefun.com

Jeez, you're a little irritable, Kyle. What's the matter, you got some sand in your vagina?

Cartman to Kyle, after the shit hits the fan,* literally, on *Cop Drama*.

Season 5, Episode 1, "It Hits the Fan"
Eric Cartman Best Quotes, southparkquotes.com

*The word "shit" is said 162 times in this episode!

[Trey and I] never have had any big blowups, because we're big enough dicks that if we did, we'd never talk again.

Matt Stone, on why his creative and business relationship with Trey Parker has endured for so long, interview with David Wild, *Rolling Stone*, January 13, 2015.